MW00905425

The Life Cycle of an

Jill Bailey

Illustrated by
Jackie Harland

Reading Consultant:
Diana Bentley

Life Cycles

Cover illustration: Jackie Harland
Editor: Janet De Saulles

First published in 1989 by
Wayland (Publishers) Limited
61 Western Road, Hove
East Sussex, BN3 1JD, England

British Library Cataloguing in Publication Data
Bailey, Jill
    The life cycle of an owl.
    1. Owls
    I. Title   II. Harland, Jackie   III. Series
    598'97

    ISBN 1–85210–622–0

Typeset in the UK by DP Press Limited, Sevenoaks, Kent
Printed and bound by Casterman S.A., Belgium

Notes for parents and teachers
Each title in this series has been specially written and
designed as a first natural history book for young readers.
For less able readers there are introductory captions,
while the more detailed text explains each illustration.

Contents

All the words that are
in **bold** are explained in
the glossary on page 31.

An owl is a bird.

All birds have wings for flying. Their
bodies are covered in feathers, and
their feet are covered in **scales**.
Instead of jaws and teeth, birds have
horny beaks with sharp edges. Owls
have soft, fluffy feathers and large
feet which are armed with sharp
claws called **talons**. The talons are
used for seizing and killing the
owl's **prey**.

Owls hunt at night and sleep by day.

Owls feed on small animals such as mice and shrews. They use their sharp, curved beaks to tear at the meat. Owls have large eyes and can see very well in the dark. They also have much better hearing than humans. Their ears are hidden behind two large circles of flattened feathers. These act as dishes which collect sounds.

The barn owl lives in barns and old buildings.

The barn owl likes places where there are plenty of mice. Each barn owl has its own special patch of countryside in which to hunt. This is its **territory**. It warns other owls to keep away by calling out as it hunts. If they come too close it will chase them away.

In spring the male owl looks for a female.

The male owl calls to attract the female. She answers with a different call and they sing together. The male may give the female a dead mouse as a present. Then he sits beside her and sways from side to side, fluffing up his feathers and flapping his wings slowly. The female cuddles up close to him and then they touch beaks.

The male and female owls **mate**.

The male owl squirts a special liquid inside the female to make her eggs grow. This liquid is called **sperm**. Now the eggs can grow inside the female owl. When each egg is big enough, a hard shell forms around it, and it is ready to be laid.

The female owl lays her eggs.

The owls find a safe place to produce their family. This may be in a barn, a church tower, or even a hole in a tall tree. The female owl does not make a proper nest. Every two or three days she lays a white egg until she has laid up to eleven eggs.

The mother owl sits on her eggs to keep them warm.

This is called **incubating**. The warmth of her body helps the young chicks to grow quickly inside the eggs. They feed on the yellow yolk in the eggs. Gradually they grow from tiny blobs to little chicks. The father owl brings food to the mother owl while she incubates the eggs.

The eggs **hatch**.

After about a month, the first egg starts to hatch. The young chick inside has a special egg tooth on its beak to help it crack the egg shell and escape. This tooth falls off soon after hatching. The other eggs hatch later because they were laid later.

The baby owls have coats of fluffy **down**.

Down is very warm. After one or two weeks, the down begins to grow thicker and turns pale brown. Seven weeks later the baby owls have a proper coat of feathers. The parent owls work hard bringing food to the chicks. The oldest, largest chick is fed first and gets the most food.

21

The young owls are ready to fly.

After about three months the young owls practise flapping their wings in order to make them strong. Then they leave home for the first time. Their parents must still feed them until they learn how to hunt.

The young owls look for new homes.

When the young owls are fully grown their parents drive them away. Their territory is not big enough to supply food for a whole family during the winter. This is a very dangerous time. The young owls must learn to avoid moving cars and to recognize their enemies.

Owls have enemies.

Owls are hunted by foxes and cats. They may fly into electricity lines, or be hit by cars. Some owls are accidentally killed by poisons used to kill insects or rats. When in danger, owls will fluff up their feathers and hiss at their enemies. Sometimes they attack with their talons.

Looking for owls.

Owls are very difficult to see because during the day they sleep, hidden in a barn or high in a tree. At night they hunt, so then you can listen for their calls. Owls also leave clues behind them. They swallow their prey whole, but they cannot **digest** the bones and fur. Instead, the bones and fur form a pellet which the owl brings back into its mouth and spits out. You can find these pellets near places where owls sleep. You may find some owl feathers, too.

owl pellet

Pygmy Owl

Snowy Owl

Burrowing Owl

The life cycle of an owl.

How many stages of the life cycle of an owl can you remember?

Glossary

Digest The food an animal eats is broken down into smaller pieces inside the animal's body. These pieces are then used to give the animal energy.

Down Soft, fluffy feathers which are very warm.

Hatch To break out of an egg.

Incubation The time spent by the mother owl sitting on the eggs to keep them warm.

Mate This is when male (father) and female (mother) animals join. It is how a baby animal is started.

Prey Animals that are killed and eaten by other animals.

Scales Hard or horny plates which protect the owl's feet.

Sperm A liquid from the male which mixes with the eggs inside the female's body. If this does not happen, the eggs will not grow.

Talons Long, curved, very sharp claws.

Territory A piece of land which an animal defends to prevent other animals using it.

Finding out more

Here are some books to read to find out more about owls.

Animals at Night by Susanna Ray (A. & C. Black, 1986)
Barn Owl by Phyllis Flower (World's Work, 1978)
Birds of Prey by Jill Bailey (Hodder & Stoughton, 1988)
The Owl in the Tree by Jennifer Coldrey
    (Methuen, 1988)
Owls by Graham Martin (A. & C. Black, 1980)

Index